The Other Way Home

Dear _Fred Clayton_ —
It has been so nice knowing
you in the Status Class all
these years while I was
finding my way home.
Fondly
Margean

The Other Way Home
A guide for seniors who live with their children

Margaret Rodgers

Asheville, NC

Published by SymPoint Communications, Inc.
Asheville, NC 28803

Publisher's Cataloging-in-Publication
(Provided by Quality Books, Inc.)

    Rodgers, Margaret, 1916-
      The other way home : a guide for seniors who live
    with their children / Margaret Rodgers.
      p. cm.
      ISBN 0-9764399-0-5
      ISBN 0-9764399-1-3

      1. Aging parents--Care--Handbooks, manuals, etc.
    2. Aging parents--Family relationships. 3. Adult children
    of aging parents--Family relationships. 4. Aging
    parents--Life skills guides. I. Title.

    HQ1063.6.R634 2004   646.7'9
                    QBI04-200522

For my children and grandchildren

Acknowledgements

My life has been so very blessed
In just about every way.
Without my partner at my side
Who could share my life each day.

My children, of course, who else would there be
To watch over me all these years?
I've written this book on staying with kids
'Cause they took away all my fears.

Researching this book has taught me a lot
About life with the next generation
And seeing how good life really can be
All around this wonderful nation.

So thanks a lot to all my family
For I have no burden to carry
When God is taking care of us
Unhappiness dares not tarry.

Contents

Who ages with grace
shall forever be young at heart

Introduction

"I'll never live with my children!" Almost a half-century after her death, I still can hear the emphatic words of my mother. In my youth, I remember wondering why such a loving and gentle woman would say such a thing. Perhaps she was reflecting the old-fashioned notion that a surviving spouse would automatically live with one of the children, whether anybody was enthusiastic about the idea or not.

What choices did widowed seniors have in those days? There were few, if any, homes for their care. Often derisively called "old folk's homes," the ones that did exist were nothing like the wonderful continuing care retirement communities we have today. But when I was growing up, family members tended stay close by their parents, and many times with their help widowed seniors could remain secure in their own homes and communities. If for some reason that was not an option, an adult child might be asked to make their home with the parent needing assistance. The last option, and the one my mother had staunchly opposed, was to join the family of an adult child in their own home. Despite her earlier objections, it became the best option for my parents when my father suddenly had a stroke just before retirement. After struggling a short time to take care of an invalid husband, Mother was greatly relieved when my sister, Janet, and her husband bought a large home and invited them to move in.

As it turned out, this would be a brief arrangement. Because of my father's failing health my mother fell into a state of depression. On her doctor's advice, she decided to take a brief trip from their home in upstate New York to visit my family in Oregon. The prospect of Mother's arrival was quite exciting, as she had not visited my family for some time, and had never seen my two infant daughters. Mother decided it would be best to admit my father to the hospital in her absence. He had been the administrator there for a number of years and she was confident that he would feel quite at home in the company of the many people he knew. In addition, she knew that Janet would check on him regularly. So she departed for her much-needed trip feeling very comfortable with the arrangements that had been made.

Our excitement was very short-lived. On the first day of her visit, an early morning phone call from Janet advised me that our father had died suddenly during the night. I never dreamed I would be the one to deliver such devastating news to our mother.

Mother immediately made plans to return home, urging me not to come with her, as I had four small children to look after. "You can come in a day or so when things settle down," she reassured me. So we put her on a short flight to California where my other sister, Louise, met and accompanied her back home to New York state. The plan was for me to follow the next day. Once again, fate would not deem it so.

As they were rushing to catch a connecting flight in

New York City, Louise noticed that Mother seemed to be out of breath. She asked, "Are you all right, Mother?" "Yes," she replied, "but I can't go any faster." If it is possible to die from a broken heart, I am sure my mother did. So consumed was she by the thought of my father dying in her absence, she herself collapsed in the airport from a fatal heart attack.

The shock of a double funeral was in direct contrast to how easy my parents had made life for us three sisters. It is difficult enough to say goodbye to a parent, but the pain of closing that chapter two times in 24 hours simply defies words.

My mother and father were only in their sixties when they died. Consequently, I was not prepared to deal with the myriad issues that surround the care of an aging parent. My dilemma would not be how to deal with my own parents, but rather how my children would deal with my care as their aging parent.

It would be nice if early in life we could look into a crystal ball and see how we would be affected by aging. If only we knew well in advance how long we would live, how much money we would have, and whether we would be blind, or stricken with physical disabilities, or struggle with cancer or heart disease. Then perhaps planning for old age would be a far simpler process. But since that is not possible, we have to prepare as best we can on all fronts. Our needs will change over time. The living arrangements I had immediately following the death of my husband are not the living arrangements I now have, and the road in between brought me many valuable experiences. In retrospect, I have gained invaluable knowledge not only about the many challenges faced by those who care for aging parents, but also how it feels to be one. My goal is to share the wisdom I have acquired through my own experience with those of you who, like me, have been given the gift of living well into your golden years.

Margaret Rodgers
December 2004

Chapter 1
The Decision

Nothing is more difficult, and therefore more precious, than to be able to decide.

Napoleon Bonaparte

The day had finally come, the day reality told me would inevitably arrive. I should have been thinking about what the future might hold, but I wasn't willing to accept the fact that such an unexpected event would happen to us. It didn't seem fair that after all those years of working and planning and raising the kids, my husband Fred wouldn't be here to enjoy our senior years together.

In December 1991, we were visiting one of our children for the holidays when Fred developed what seemed to be a bad cold. We rushed back home to Dallas so he could consult his regular doctor. As his symptoms pointed to pneumonia, the doctor immediately admitted him to the hospital. Although he was not a smoker, the next day he was diagnosed with inoperable lung cancer and given only six months to live.

Despite this crushing blow, Fred was back home very soon, appearing to feel just fine. His diagnosis seemed rather surreal, as nothing in his outward appearance had changed. I must admit that in my mind I was even denying the possibility of his having cancer. Over the next few weeks, we traveled around visiting friends and relatives in many places from coast to coast. But my optimism was short-lived, for after six months had elapsed, it was apparent that his disease was catching up to him.

The children and their families all came for Thanksgiving that year. Even though Fred was on oxygen and in a wheel chair, he was determined to carve the turkey with the same precision that had been our family tradition for over forty years. The next day toward late afternoon he became totally exhausted, so we helped him to bed where he looked at me with outstretched arms and said "I'm so glad I married you." Having been surrounded by his entire family for three days, he died peacefully later that evening. The day I had been dreading for over nine months had finally arrived.

I suddenly found myself strangely alone, devastated by the prospect of life without my partner of 47 years. Our four children were all married, all immersed in their own lives with kids and carpools and soccer games, just as I had been at their ages. Moreover, they were scattered about the country like windblown seeds, the closest living almost 300 miles away.

But an even more painful reality awaited me. A few years earlier, I had been diagnosed with macular degeneration, the leading cause of blindness in people over age 65. My sharp-as-a-tack eyesight was failing, and during this most difficult period of transition, I was declared legally blind. Driving became a distant memory, and with no one to chauffeur me around as my husband had so willingly done, my life abruptly came to a complete standstill.

In the emptiness of the home where so many wonderful memories—holidays, birthdays, graduations and anniversaries—had been created, a feeling of despair washed over me, the loneliness at times too great to bear.

Fortunately, my children came to the rescue. They

proposed an interesting plan: sell my house, and rotate around by staying with each of them for three months out of the year.

"What a wonderful idea, so comforting and so refreshing!" I thought. To always have family around who would be there whenever I needed them seemed like a great idea.   Besides, I had never been one to let grass grow under my feet. This plan would mean my time would be divided between Georgia, Florida, and Texas each year, and that I could now be a firsthand witness to the fascinating antics of my 10 grandchildren. It sounded like a perfect solution, yet the little voice inside cautioned me not plant that "for sale" sign in the front yard just yet. This idea would need some serious consideration.

Then I remembered a conversation I had with my husband a few years earlier. We were wondering just how we would spend our "twilight years," hoping we could be free from the responsibility of caring for a home which was far larger than our needs required. We also wanted to maintain close ties with our children, but knew the chances of their living in the same city we did were slim. Arranging reunions was becoming more and more difficult as each family was on a different schedule. Then too, there was always the question of whether or not our children wanted to spend their precious vacation time visiting parents.

So the two of us dreamed up a great plan. We would rent a vacation home in an exciting place large enough to accommodate visiting children and grandchildren, living there part of each year while entertaining a houseful of relatives and friends. When the vacation season ended, we would travel and visit each of our children and their families for whatever time was available. It would be the perfect way to keep in close touch with everyone, no matter how far away they might live.

We must have mentioned our idea to our children at some point, perhaps shortly before Fred became ill. Remembering it as I did that day helped to reassure me that their proposed plan, though somewhat modified from the original, just might work.

There were so many decisions with which I was faced. My failing vision meant that remaining in my home would be difficult at best. But the prospect of entering a retirement home alone wasn't exactly what I wanted. I guess I just hadn't owned up to my age, because when I had mentioned that I really didn't want to live with a lot of "old people," one of my daughters quipped, "Mom, have you looked in the mirror lately?"

Most of my friends had echoed my mother's sentiments about living with children. "Live with your children?" they'd say. "You poor thing, be careful with that one!"

Then I started thinking, "To whom do I want to talk for the rest of my life? Young, vibrant families about their activities, or older folks about the past?" But was I really ready for these active, bigger-than-life families? For boisterous teenagers as they stumbled into adulthood? For the fast-paced world of computers and cell phones, to say nothing of the advanced ideas and concepts to which I would be exposed? It was a far cry from my present world or even from the one in which I brought up my children. Wouldn't a retirement home perhaps be a better option?

I started to feel as if I had a devil on one shoulder and an angel on the other. My devilish little voice of skepticism chimed in, warning me about my lack of experience in being with older adults who were alone in the world. She further cautioned me about a move to unfamiliar surroundings so soon after my husband's death. Maybe I'd better just stay put, she warned, because although lonely, at least my life here was a known quantity. I could manage somehow.

Then my guardian angel had her say, reminding me that I have moved to different areas before and always managed to keep my old friends and acquaintances while making new ones. "Besides," her little voice persuaded, "if you live with your children, you already know some of their friends and associates. If you stay where you are, what will happen to you now that you no longer fit in with your couples friends when they get together? Will you be happy with a 'fill- in' companion? Will you be happy without your music-loving husband when you attend the concerts for which you still hold season's tickets? But most of all won't you be upset by all those memories that you can't seem to shake? They are in every corner of this house."

In the end, it was not difficult to know what I really preferred. Clearly, remaining at home alone and isolated was not an attractive option. I knew that I would much rather be close to my family, to those with whom I had strong ties. That was certainly preferable to enlisting the aid of strangers in an unfamiliar place should I need assistance. Since what my children were proposing was not so different from what Fred and I had come up with several years earlier, I felt that he was somehow giving his blessing to the idea.

So I packed up my grief and sorrow, and, leaving my loneliness behind, began an uncharted voyage to witness first-hand the good things about living with adult children and whether all the bad things I had heard were really true. It would be, to say the very least, an eye-opening journey of self-discovery.

Chapter 2
Making A Smooth Transition

Any change, even a change for the better, is always accompanied by drawbacks and discomforts.
Arnold Bennett

If your children have offered you a space within their home, it is paramount that you discuss logistics with them before the first suitcase ever crosses the threshold. Few families will have extra space just waiting to be used, so you will need to address several issues, the first of which is whether there is room for you. If so, where?

Personally, I never wanted the situation to arise where a grandchild was displaced from a bedroom because "Grandma is coming." I felt this would be starting with one strike against me. When I talk to others who are contemplating this living arrangement, particularly newly widowed women, their plaintive cry is often, "How do you handle this? A grandmother can't exactly make her bed on the living room sofa!" I agree, but not just for Grandma's sake. The truth is that moving in with your children, even if only for a few months at a time, has a huge impact on everyone in the family. If Grandmother is not too happy about making her bed on the living room sofa, that goes doubly for the teens who want to watch a movie at 3 a.m. So, you must all work together to determine exactly what your "space" will consist of, and that the arrangement is amenable to everyone.

There are options available to you if space is tight. When I decided to move in with my children, I sold my home and divided the proceeds among all four. Each one was then given the funds necessary to create a space that would not only accommodate my needs, but those of their family as well. Though it was not easy leaving my home of almost 30 years, it was clear that we would all benefit in the long run if I used the money in that way. If you are not ready or able to take such a permanent step, consider a trial run for three months or so to see how things are working. Even if you have decided to move in with a child, but still can't bear the thought of parting with your house, talk to a realtor about the possibility of leasing your property. Many of us have been in our homes for such a long time that we can rent them out for substantially more than the cost of a mortgage payment, if in fact we still have one. If you do not own a home, you are in an even better position to try this out for a few months, because you can then end your lease (or not) depending on how well it works for you.

In just about any scenario, you can use the money that you are not paying to a mortgage company or landlord to help finance the creation of a suitable space in your child's home. Nor does this have to be a major construction project that costs thousands of dollars. You may need to think outside the box to come up with an arrangement that works, but it can be done. Try to be open-minded and creative during this process.

Space-smart ideas such as Murphy beds abound these days, and there is no shortage of talented and creative designers who can conjure up innovative solutions to just about any "we need more room" dilemma. There is also a relatively new solution to the where-to-put-mom problem, which is called ECHO (Elder Cottage Housing Opportunities.) It is a temporary, movable and low-cost self-contained house designed to enable older persons to live on the same property as their family without living under the same roof.

Whatever your particular living arrangement, the key is for everyone involved to remain flexible, and in so doing, you will all benefit in the long run. The extra space created for you can be used by other family members when you are away, and will undoubtedly enhance the value of the home in which you are living.

Your new space will most likely be smaller than the one from which you are moving, particularly if you are coming out of your own home. So what happens to all your things? This is perhaps one of the greatest material benefits of living with your children. You won't necessarily have to bid farewell to all those treasures you have acquired over the years. You will appreciate seeing most of your possessions in your new surroundings.

What worked best for me was to pack up my personal belongings, then let my children divvy up the rest. It was fascinating to see who wanted what, but I stayed out of the fray and instead let thcm negotiate their own deals, with one exception. Since I was disposing of some rather large-ticket items, such as a baby grand piano and a car, I tried to ensure that each child received something of equal value from those more high-dollar possessions. Depending on the number of children, step-children, etc. that you have, you may want to enlist the help of an appraiser in this process. Beyond that, the children worked off of my "master" list, putting their initials on things they wanted. When two or more wanted a single item, it was up to them to barter with one another. The list proved to be a great way to streamline an otherwise insurmountable task.

Nowadays, in this age of "digital everything," there is an even better way to divide your belongings. I recommend that you take digital photos of all your goods and print them out. Your children or grandchildren can probably do this if you do not know how. Circulate the pictures among your children so they can decide who gets what and dispose of the rest. I hired an estate sale company to tag and sell anything that was left over from our cumulative list, and pocketed a tidy sum to boot. After all was said and done, I got the best of both worlds, giving what they wanted to my children, and generating some quick cash for the leftovers. I also made it clear to my children that when something they selected for their home no longer worked for them, then they were free to sell, donate, or dispose of it however they saw fit. Frankly, I was surprised how easy it was to let go of material possessions that I had owned for years, and in the end I realized that it was actually a tremendous relief not to have to keep up with so many things!

A word of caution here. Although many of your things may end up in your new "home," you must be aware that the memories you have attached to a particular object do necessarily not transfer to your children. I was shocked one Halloween when my granddaughter used a beautiful sterling silver bowl we had received as a wedding gift as the "trick or treat" candy dish. This particular piece had been given to us by the widow of the owner of the company for which my husband worked as a young man. It was indicative of the high esteem in which he was held by all who knew him there, and for that reason I used it only on very special occasions. Upon reflection, I realized that the history of an item is often more precious than its value, and therefore there was nothing wrong with my granddaughter using the dish in the way she had chosen. The same situation is true in reverse. When we were cleaning out my home, I almost gave away an old wool blanket only to learn that it was highly sought after by my two younger daughters, both of whom had fond childhood memories of it!

Once you've waded through the sea of belongings you've accumulated over your lifetime, divvied them up to everyone's satisfaction, and located your corner of the earth in your child's home, you are ready to move in and move on to an even more pressing issue: money, that ever-present and necessary fact of life.

Chapter 3
Money Matters, In Many Ways

*Money is power, freedom, a cushion, the root of
all evil, the sum of blessings.*

Carl Sandburg

I came into the world just prior to the great depression of 1929, so this period undoubtedly influenced my thinking. To this day, one of my sons-in-law teases me about my "depression mentality!"

That having been said, should you be contemplating an extended visit with your children, one of the most important issues you need to discuss is money, specifically who is planning to pay for what.

Faced with the prospect of liquidating most of your worldly possessions to move in with a child will undoubtedly prompt the question, "What about all my retirement years? If I part with my house and all my furniture, will I be secure with the other resources I have?"

The news media is constantly reminding us about the cost of retirement, and the fact that the government's Social Security program was never intended to supply all of our retirement income. It was only intended to serve as a supplement to an individual retirement plan already in place.

Because the cost of maintaining one person in a separate home can be significant, pooling some resources through extended family living can be very beneficial, especially now that life expectancy is getting longer. It might not be long before "extended family living" turns into "extended financial savings" and security and peace of mind for everyone, as financing aging parents into their senior years is also of concern to children who may become burdened with this task when resources run out.

Once you have moved in with your child, one of the first details to be addressed is the question of on-going expenses for items such as utilities, long distance phone calls, and food. The money I initially gave my children was used to create a physical space in which I could live, and was not intended to cover daily living expenses. Although these day-to-day expenses will most likely be very small, it is important to make some gesture of willingness to pay your fair share. In my situation, I did not want to ask how much my portion of the bill was every time we went out, nor did I expect the children to always pick up the tab. So I proposed a monthly subsidy that would more than take care of all my maintenance-type expenses. This way I felt free to ask for some special grocery store item, such as a tube of toothpaste or a favorite snack. It is amazing how much this gesture is appreciated, whether verbalized or not, and it can make things easier and happier for everyone. In addition, I occasionally treated the family to a meal out, usually on some special occasion.

Some people will move in with their children simply because their finances do not leave them any other option. If your personal finances are tight and you do not have the resources to contribute to the household, offer to help out in some way that is appreciated such as cooking dinner on occasion, watching the kids for an hour or two, or anything that works in your family situation. The type of contribution, financial or otherwise, is not nearly as important as your willingness to offer some form of assistance.

There will be some routine costs for which you should budget when living with your children. Although they will vary according to the person, they most likely will include things such as life and health insurance, medications, clothing, travel costs, organizational memberships and charitable contributions. Most of these items are probably things you already pay for each month, but they should definitely be reviewed when you change your living arrangements.

What about your bank account and personal funds? How will you access these when you move in with a child? This depends a lot on whether or not you are moving out of the city in which you have been living. If not, you can probably leave things just as they are. If you are moving to another state or rotating around as I did, you may want to choose one home and make it your permanent address. I chose the child who had the most space for me to leave my permanent files. Selecting a permanent address is a must for all legal documents, including Social Security and Medicare accounts, tax forms, insurance policies, driver's license or identification card, passport, etc. Having one permanent address ensures that financial statements, tax information, credit card bills and other essential information will always come to one place. In these days of rampant identity theft, make sure that you shred any documents you do not need. Your children may already own a shredder, but if not, they are affordable and do not take up much space.

With regard to finances, even if you move out-of-state, you may still be able to keep the same checking account by taking advantage of the government's direct deposit program for Social Security checks and using a debit card that immediately drafts your bank account, wherever it may be, when you make a purchase. Pre-authorized bank drafts in which a company secures your permission to automatically debit your checking account in the amount and on the date of your choosing can also be established for fixed expenses such as insurance premiums. Those of us with internet savvy can easily pay bills on-line from any location, which cuts down tremendously on paperwork! Check with your bank for more information about on-line banking, and be sure to notify them of your change of address, even if you keep the same account.

If you will be staying with multiple families, it is probably a good idea to have a renter's insurance policy to cover all your personal belongings. Your children may have insurance that will cover any property loss you might incur while with them, so be sure to check this out. Some credit card companies now include insurance coverage for losses sustained while traveling if you have paid for your trip with their credit card. Check with your credit card company to determine what is covered should you incur some sort of loss while traveling from one location to another.

If you travel between states as I did, you will need to consider where your professional advisors will be. These are people such as an attorney, financial adviser, stock broker, accountant, and the like. You may not have a need for all of these people, but if you do, try to choose them in the state of your permanent address. I once encountered difficulty trying to do business with a stock broker in one state where I was visiting, because he was not licensed to do business in the state of my permanent residence. Be aware that licensing restrictions can occur in many of the above professions.

Ironing out the financial details on all of these fronts will avoid confusion, misunderstandings and time-consuming discussions down the road. Your attention to detail in these matters early-on will yield great dividends in the years to come.

Chapter 4
Finding the Perfect Fit

Learn from yesterday, live for today,
hope for tomorrow.
Anonymous

It's a huge adjustment for our adult children, most of whom are "baby boomers", to have Mom, Dad, or both come to stay for extended visits. Our children are often referred to as the "sandwich generation," because they are squeezed in between caring for their own children and for their aging parents. There is no doubt that these middle-aged adults have a far different role to play in this fast-changing world than we knew when we were their age.

We are all familiar with mother-in-law jokes that portray us as constantly making derisive comments. Indeed, there is a gray area between offering what we feel is time-honored wisdom and what is interpreted by others as harsh criticism. Hopefully your children (and children-in-law) will let you know if you are going overboard with advice.

One thing we need to remember is that our children may have selected a partner whose background and experiences are quite different from their own, and these differences will factor into the couple's decision making. We are so accustomed to calling the shots in our own households, it is often difficult to get out of the habit and let go of the reins. It is now time for our children to reign over their own kingdoms.

So what is the best way to "fit in" when you live with your children? My advice is simple: go with the flow. By that I mean that you must all work together to forge out a viable living arrangement. For some families, this will mean that your input is welcomed in everything; for others, it will mean that you will be asked when and if your advice or assistance is needed.

The key is to keep the lines of communication open. Talk to one another regularly, discussing your feelings, needs, and desires and whether or not everyone thinks the arrangement is working. Sweeping emotionally charged issues under the rug will only backfire later on when someone reaches the boiling point. For everyone's sake, don't let this happen. I wish I could have skipped that first year and started in the second year with all the knowledge I had accumulated over the previous twelve months. It would have spared a lot of hurt feelings.

It will take time to sort out this new living equation, and it will vary across families. If you run into tricky issues that seem impossible to resolve, seek the assistance of a counselor, minister, or social worker who can offer advice about how to ease the situation. Had my children and I done this, it might have made the transition a bit smoother in those early years.

Sometimes the transition into a home is complicated by the fact that many women are no longer at home during the day. Juggling a career and family can be quite stressful, and this must be taken into account when discussing an extended-family living arrangement. Often women feel the obligation of being the primary caretaker of an elderly parent, whether that is anyone's intent or not. Make sure that this issue is discussed openly and honestly with your children so that everyone is clear and in agreement about how you will merge into the family.

With regard to household chores, most of us don't want to move in and become the full-time maid, butler, nanny, chauffeur or cook. We've earned our stripes in those areas earlier in life. But it is nice to offer to help, and even if it is refused, don't be offended. It was to my great relief that my daughters politely declined my offer to help prepare meals, as my eyesight was so poor that I could no longer see well enough not to get a tablespoon of salt in a recipe that needed only a pinch. Instead, I opted to set the table and clear it after the meals, which was most appreciated by some rather weary working parents.

Be careful not to do anything around the house unless specifically asked. A lot of your "tidying up" will not be appreciated if you move things into a location where they can't be found. It might open the doorway for hurt feelings, as your actions may be interpreted as a sign that you do not think your children are capable of keeping things in order. I remember the time I decided clean out my daughter's pantry, which seemed an awful mess. Although the family was very polite about it, I could tell that they would have preferred not to have the pantry reorganized, as they were used to reaching for things in a certain place.

The most important thing to remember is that blending into a family takes time, patience, and tolerance. If you step on some toes in the process, own up to it and move on. If your toes get stepped on, do your best to let it go. Remembering who-said-what-and-hurt-whose-feelings will only undermine the creation of a peaceable kingdom that, at the end of the day, everyone needs in their home.

Chapter 5
Living with Teens

*Few things are more satisfying than seeing your
children have teenagers of their own.*

Doug Larson, Olympic Medalist

Probably the biggest adjustment I had to make when living with my children was learning how to bridge the generation gap so I could relate to my teenage grandchildren. Well into my 70s at the time of my move-in, these young people were more than half a century my junior. I had difficulty understanding their language, to say nothing of their dress and demeanor. Theirs was an electronic world of fast-paced cell phones, video games and computers about which I knew nothing.

The first few months of living with teens were akin to what my youngest daughter affectionately refers to as "the clash of the Titans." I could not relate to their lives, nor they to mine. One of my children recalls the stress of running interference between two generations with a gap "as wide as the ocean." I had been concerned about this before I decided to move in, but had not been prepared for just how challenging this might be.

I think it is fair to say that most of us will find that today's young people are growing up during a technological revolution that is immeasurably different from our teenage years. In my early days, just owning a telephone was a luxury that few could afford. As a child, I remember visiting my grandmother who had a telephone mounted on her wall. It had a handle which could be cranked to ring up the operator, who was almost like a private secretary, for she knew where everyone in town was and could usually reach the party needed provided they were near a phone. When Fred and I married just after World War II, we lived in a small town and could not get anything but a "four party" telephone line, a single line which served four different households, each with a distinctive ring. Coming from that background, it was difficult to imagine a world in which my grandchildren would carry a phone – their own personal number, no less – in their purse or pocket!

Initially, communicating one-on-one with my teenage grandchildren was difficult at best. I found they would either talk my ear off or not speak to me at all. I felt frustrated by a generation who did not show the respect for elders I had learned at their age, and who used language to which I could not relate. Yet these were not "problem" kids who got into trouble, quite the contrary. In fact, my most turbulent relationship was with a grandson who was well liked and graduated near the top of his high school class.

I think one of my biggest challenges in those days was figuring out just how I could fit in to the teenage world. I wanted to share in their lives, but often felt that they perceived my questions and comments as meddling or judgmental. Those toddler days when they would crawl into my lap and give me big hugs were clearly a thing of the past. Worse yet, I quickly found that when there was conflict, their parents usually did not back me up, but instead supported their own children's viewpoints. What to do?

It was clear that there was no way such polarized exchanges would benefit any of us. So, I began to reframe my views. Yes, these kids were very different from what I remembered of my youth, and granted, I did not like some of what I was seeing. But by looking beyond that, I was able to see the tremendous resource that was right under my nose. For example, when I wanted to learn how to use a computer, several of my grandchildren were on the scene to help me navigate the cyber world (not to mention my only son who, to this day, is my constant savior.) Faced with the challenge of keeping my files with me when traveling from family to family, one grandson quickly pointed out that by purchasing a laptop, I could easily do just that. He immediately researched the most current equipment and price, helping me to select the best fit for my needs. All this at age 13!

What I began to realize is just how exposed to the world—good, bad, and otherwise—these young people are. Their instant access to events around the globe is a stark contrast to the days when I had to go to the movies to see the latest trends in fashion and style. Granted, we are not going to return to our world of yesterday, so that only leaves one option: hang on to your hat and enjoy the ride into their world of today. My advice on how to do that is to listen. Period. Sincerely, earnestly listen to what your teenage grandchildren are saying. Be open and receptive to their attitudes and opinions, even when they differ from your own. Some days they may be more communicative than others. Take that at face value, for if you are really a good listener, most likely their silence will not be directed at you.

Gaining your grandchildren's confidence as a sounding board will enable you to bridge a huge generation gap, as these young people are your gateway to the world as it now exists. Yes, you will see strange trends, fads that come and go, hairstyles and foods and phrases and music that you don't recognize, but why not enjoy the novelty? If you hunker down in your own values, you will completely miss watching them forge out theirs. You don't have to agree with or like everything they do, but simply respect these developing young adults for who they are. You will reap enormous benefits. And you will probably find, as I did, that once they realize you are not opposed to everything they say and do they will become much more open to what you have to say.

As they grow in wisdom and stature, your teenage grandchildren will learn to appreciate the loving relationship which has always been there for them. That grandson with whom I was apt to lock horns? When I began to listen and respect him, things changed. Now, every so often, the phone rings and I hear a well mannered and mature voice on the other end of the line. He calls just to check in and tell me about his life, and find out about mine. It truly makes my day.

Chapter 6
Traditions: Yours, Mine, Ours

*What an enormous magnifier is tradition! How a
thing grows in the human memory and in the human
imagination, when love, worship, and all that lies
in the human heart, is there to encourage it.*

Thomas Carlyle 1795-1881

Merging into an existing household means combining old and new traditions. It will take some effort on everyone's part to establish a new routine that works. There are four areas relevant to this topic which warrant further discussion: meals, the family hierarchy, phones and worship. Addressing these areas when you first move in will ensure smooth sailing down the road.

In my youth, meals were a time of lively family discussion and conversation, particularly after church on Sundays. I recall stories about the great conversations that were held at the dinner table while my father was growing up. The youngest of seven children, he had six brothers, some of whom followed my grandfather's path into the clergy. Although my grandfather died before I was born, the legacy of the wonderful family stories that were told in that home still persists. These stories provided me with invaluable information about my ancestors and also about the way of life in bygone days.

When I moved in with my children, it was very hard for me to adjust to whirlwind family meals in which my grandchildren would gulp down their food and leave the table. My youngest daughter, sympathetic to my struggle with the mealtime hustle-bustle, used to tease me by saying she would just put a trough on the table so we could slurp up our food without having to sit down. It saddened me that such a wonderful opportunity to share the family lore was being missed, not to mention the special Sunday dinners complete with china and sterling that we enjoyed with our children as they were growing up.

A few years after I began living with my children, I realized that often issues like this will iron themselves out over time. Two of my grandchildren who "ate and ran" later studied in Europe, and each came home with a newfound admiration for long conversations at mealtime, as is the custom in many countries abroad. Meals became a time for lively—and I do mean lively—political discussions, family stories, and comparisons of modern-day life with my often-humorous memories of how things were some sixty-odd years ago.

In addition to adjusting to the way meals are eaten, you may also have to adjust to the foods themselves. When you are not the cook, as was the case with me, you may need to modify your dietary choices. I had to adapt to eating many foods to which I was not accustomed, and become flexible in my food preferences. I have always been a fresh vegetable lover, because when I graduated from college, I worked at a school for delinquent girls where all the foods were grown on-site. We had a dietician who never served less than four or five fresh vegetables with every meal, so I became completely enamored of the range and variety of fresh foods available from the plant kingdom, and my cooking over the years reflected this preference. However, I did not work outside the home until after my children were grown, so I had much more time to prepare meals from fresh ingredients than any of my working children.

If you have specific dietary restrictions, you may

face more of a challenge. For example, perhaps you are a devout beef lover who moves in with a vegetarian child—or vice versa. In addition, ethnic foods that may be unfamiliar to you are now much more common as dinner entrees. Work together with your child to find a solution, either by fixing separate foods that meet your requirements, or modifying existing recipes to suit your needs. I advise the latter if at all possible. Eating separately prepared foods is much more work for everyone, and is not in the community spirit that is so important at mealtime.

During the many years I lived with my children, I was never once served anything I felt that I could not eat. In fact, I enjoyed the wide variety that existed between each of my four children's households. Should you encounter something you don't like, refrain from displaying your disapproval. Nothing is more annoying than spending time preparing a meal only to be met with criticism. Save your comments for the things you do like, and freely compliment the chef! If you are still able to cook, your children may relish having you prepare the old favorites, or trying your hand at some new ones. There were many times when my children would ask how I made cookies or other desserts, or a certain casserole that they remembered from their youth.

The family hierarchy can be another challenging area. Exactly where do we as aging parents fit into the picture? Just because you are a member of the household does not necessarily mean that you should insert yourself into every conversation, so exercise discretion when expressing your opinions during family discussions. At first, it was hard for me to refrain from asking who-was-going-where-and-when-and-why, but I quickly learned it was not appreciated when I asked too many questions. I realized that I did not need to know all the details of an event and that it was preferable to being too inquisitive. There is a fine line between not intruding on your host family, yet demonstrating an interest in their thoughts and activities. This is one of the most difficult distinctions you will have to make, and it is complicated by the fact that you will probably have to cross that line a few times in order to learn just where it is.

It is also important to allow your host family to have their own privacy. Give them the space to function as they would were you not there by occasionally keeping busy in your own quarters. When sparks fly between any members of the household, try to remain out of the fray. And, no matter what transpires within a family, never communicate your disapproval with the actions of one of your adult children to their siblings. Chances are good they will share that information with one another, and no one will benefit in the long run. If it is necessary for you to vent about something that has happened, call a friend who is willing to be a good listener while you get it off your chest.

Remember, too, that your days of child rearing are over, and that your children are now in charge of their own households. Let them be the disciplinarians, unless you have specifically been asked to intervene. This can be tricky, especially when you are home with grandkids whose parents are out.

I remember visiting my daughter's family at a time when her three children were all in their teens. Confident that the kids were old enough to watch over themselves, she and her husband went out for a meal at a nearby restaurant. While they were away, all three kids decided to bleach their otherwise brown hair to a buttery golden blonde. I was completely at a loss for what to do, not having visited this family in a few months. I wondered if my daughter would arrive home and become irate that I had allowed such a thing to transpire right before my eyes. On the other hand, I was not officially in charge, so felt it inappropriate to start mandating what my grandchildren could and could not do. When I mentioned my concerns to the kids, they said their parents would not object, so I let it go. It turns out they were right. When my daughter walked in the door, she looked at her three newly coiffed kids and proclaimed, "Wow, I love it!" Obviously, I was quite relieved, especially when she later told me that she could certainly understand my dilemma!

One of the biggest transitions I had to make when I moved in with my children was in relation to the telephone. It was terribly difficult for me to accept the fact that when the phone rang it was rarely for me. After all, in my house it had *always* been for me. It was also hard to adjust to sharing a message machine with others, many of whom did not necessarily want me to listen to their personal messages while searching for my own. Then there were other times that someone took a message but forgot to give it to me.

Fortunately, the world of technology now offers some great solutions for these problems. First, ask your children to check with the phone company to see if they offer what is called a "distinctive ring." This is a series of short rings that sound slightly different from a regular phone ring. Most phone companies offer this with a unique phone number that actually "rides" over the existing phone line. In some cases, this service is available at no additional charge, and it enables you to have your own personal telephone number that can be given out to friends and businesses. In areas where this in not available, you might do what I did. I settled on a system where my friends would call, let it ring twice, and then hang up and call right back. It was my way of knowing that most likely the call was for me.

Worship is another area that needs to be addressed. Having worship as part of our lives is certainly a great comfort and joy as we age. It is becoming commonplace to hear members of the medical community discuss the positive impact of worship and prayer on our physical well being.

As your children age and marry, they may adopt new religious affiliations. Don't be upset or surprised should they elect to follow a tradition other than the one in which you raised them. Rejoice that they have taken the initiative to forge out their own spiritual paths. All four of my children elected to join either another denomination of church or a different type of religion entirely. I not only join them in attending their services, but I have acquired a significant understanding of their choices. I respect their traditions and they mine, as they will often accompany me in services at my church as well.

Mutual respect is the most important factor in establishing new traditions. From something as trivial as who answers the phone to something as vital as family worship, respect plays a major role in charting a course that can be smoothly navigated by all.

Chapter 7
You've Moved In, So Get Moving!

*Life is like riding a bicycle. To keep your
balance you must keep moving.*
                                    Albert Einstein

So you've taken the plunge, consolidated your household, transferred your bank statements changed your address and are finally settled in with your family. Great! Now what? Transitioning to a new living arrangement will most likely be stressful for everyone, most of all you. While other family members are marching on through their daily routines, you may feel alone and unsure what to do because at the moment, your life is anything but routine. Why not seize this tremendous opportunity to create some new habits?

One of the best ways to begin your day is through some form of exercise. It's hard to open a magazine or listen to a newscast without seeing something that extols the merits of getting in shape. There is great truth to the old adage "a body in motion stays in motion." When I turned 60, I told myself "think 16." When I became 70, I thought "17", then came 80, and you guessed it.

Starting the day with exercise helps each of us physically, mentally and spiritually. Continuous exercise is especially beneficial on those days when you are feeling a little down. It increases the production and release of endorphins—neurotransmitters in the brain that provide a sort of natural "high." Even if you take no more than a short walk down the block or a stroll around the yard, you should do something every day.

In some communities there are groups of people called "mall walkers" who are interested in walking for exercise. These are usually seniors who meet in a mall at a designated time and place to walk a specified route. As it is inside, it takes place regardless of the weather. Some groups even end their walk by having coffee or a late breakfast. This is a wonderful way to meet people who have interests similar to yours. Inquire at a mall near you to see if there is such a group there, or better yet, consider starting a group in your neighborhood for outdoor walks when the weather will permit.

Regular walks that can be taken at any time or place, for as long as you choose, can't be surpassed as an effective and inexpensive program of exercise. Walking also has another great benefit: it affords us time to be alone and think without interruption, and to reflect on our spiritual faith.

When walking or exercising alone, particularly by venturing out in areas surrounding your neighborhood, never leave home without some form of identification that tells who you are, where you live, and who to contact in case of an emergency. This is sound advice for everyone, but it goes doubly for seniors.

A few years ago on one of my trips to Miami, I enrolled in a seniors' college writing class. Rather than bother my daughter who had her hands full with two small children, I walked a few blocks to the University where the class was held. I usually got a ride home from my teacher, who lived nearby, but one afternoon, I decided I'd walk home. A few minutes into the walk, I began to feel a bit odd. It was a hot summer day, and I remember thinking if I could just get out of the sun for a moment, I'd be fine. I was wrong. I blacked out, falling to the pavement. Thank goodness a woman saw me go down and called for help. But there was another problem: I had no identification on me, so it was anyone's guess who I was. After a closer look at my face, the woman said she thought she had seen me coming out of a nearby house on occasion. Fortunately, she was right, and someone went to my daughter's house to let her know the situation. It was the last time I ever left home without proper identification, and I was extremely lucky to have had no permanent injuries while learning a very valuable lesson.

For those who want a more varied exercise routine, consider joining a local health club, gymnasium or the YMCA. Most of these places have personal trainers who will design a specific regimen that fits your needs. Be sure to get your doctor's advice on what is appropriate before beginning, however. If you are on a tight budget, check with a local community center, which may offer programs for seniors free of charge.

If you are confined to a bed or wheelchair, whether

temporarily or permanently, do not despair. There are exercises you can do while sitting in a chair or even lying in bed. There are many pamphlets and books written on this subject. Perhaps a member of your host family can check with the local library, do an internet search, or contact your doctor's office for more information.

Don't forget that mental exercise is equally as important as physical exercise. Crossword puzzles and other brain teasers are a good way to keep your mind ship-shape. Just as a body in motion stays in motion, so, too, does our "gray matter" need to be used regularly.

No matter how you choose to exercise, whether in a group or alone, be sure to pace yourself. If you have not been in the habit of regular exercise, start in slowly. Being prudent will ensure that you reap the tremendous benefits of exercise while protecting your muscles, bones and joints.

Chapter 8
Reach Out and Touch Someone

Communication leads to community, that is,
to understanding, intimacy and mutual valuing.
Rollo May

Everyone likes to feel that they are contributing to life in some way, and it is essential that you take steps to honor that feeling the minute you get settled into your new quarters. Maybe you have a special talent that your family would appreciate. Perhaps you play an instrument or have a hobby and are willing to share your expertise. In my generation, women were excellent homemakers and cooks, and a good many men were quite proficient at doing handyman jobs or handling barbequing chores. I have yet to meet a family who doesn't welcome those talents. Whatever your particular area of expertise, share it with those around you. They'll no doubt be delighted that you did.

A recent university study found that seniors who are treated like they are competent, productive members of society tend to perform that way too. This brings up a critical issue about living with your children. Specifically, do not isolate yourself, as there is nothing that will contribute to depression more rapidly than the feelings of loneliness that result from not engaging with others. Most of us who live with our children are probably doing so because we have lost a spouse, or other circumstances make it impossible to live alone. The thought of venturing out to make new friends at this time in our lives is often not terribly appealing, especially if we have had to leave familiar friends and surroundings behind in another city.

This is when your attitude towards your new life becomes most important. Even if your situation is not ideal, reframing your view of it can open the doorway to seeing things in a more positive light. Scientists have proven that people with a positive attitude are significantly less likely to show signs of frailty than those who are pessimistic. It's nice to know that a little attitude adjustment can improve your health as well!

Even if you are willing to try meeting new people, what's the best way to do that? Those who drive will have little difficulty finding ways to connect with others. There is no shortage of volunteer opportunities, including tutoring in the local schools. There are also community senior centers, church groups, bridge clubs etc. Nowadays, classes for seniors are plentiful in most cities. If you opt to take a class, try a subject that is new to you. Don't be afraid to stretch your boundaries a little and move out of your comfort zone. That was exactly how I discovered my love for writing, and it has opened up an entirely new world for me. For the truly adventurous, you can now even combine learning with travel to faraway exotic places thanks to organizations like Elderhostel that cater specifically to seniors.

If all these things sound tempting but you don't drive, do not despair. I have not driven in over twelve years, but I manage to get everywhere I want to go. Although I don't need a cab very often, I was pleased to learn that some cab drivers will give you their cell phone number so that you can call them directly to arrange for a pick up.

If you do not wish to travel by cab, don't be bashful about asking for a ride from someone you know.

I recently had the opportunity to attend a seniors' college course about jazz great Dave Brubeck that was being taught by a man who had worked closely with him. As much as I wanted to attend the class, it would mean that my daughter would have to take and pick me up each day, as no other form of transportation was available. When I approached her about this, I discovered that not only was she willing, she insisted that I go!

Over time, I have gotten much better about asking for rides to church events, the hairdresser, and various meetings and classes. Much to my delight, many times when I arranged for a ride, the driver would routinely plan on picking me up for the next meeting of the same group.

If you have a limitation of some sort, be realistic about what you can and cannot do, but don't give up altogether. Just work around it. My poor eyesight meant that my bridge days were over, as were a host of other visually-oriented tasks. So, I decided that I'd capitalize on my nemesis, and became a resource person for others who were also suffering from macular degeneration. I conducted a low vision class at my church, and was even asked to sit on a state board.

If meeting new people is hard for you, remember that most people really enjoy talking about themselves. Nor must you find an extrovert in order to strike up a conversation. Many years ago I attended a rather dull banquet and was seated next to a very quiet man who was obviously a little bored as well. I decided to see if I could engage him in conversation only to discover that he was a forest ranger who jumped from airplanes to fight forest fires. He was certainly one of the most fascinating dinner companions I had ever had. I soon realized that most of us are delighted to talk about our lives, and that asking someone what "field" they are in or have been in brings out all sorts of interesting information.

There are some projects you can get involved in right at home. The explosion of technology over the last few years has given us an opportunity to use computers and e-mail to keep in touch with our friends and family who are not nearby. If you do use a computer, it's very easy to compose a letter of a few paragraphs that you plan to send to everyone, telling of your personal activities and thoughts. Then you can add individual paragraphs to start and close each letter to personalize it. You will be amazed at how little time it takes to write letters using this system. It is a lifesaver during the holiday season!

One of the things I like most about having a computer is that it enables me to easily edit my writing. Gone are the days of typewriters, carbon paper, and globs of white out. I found that of all the things I have written over the years, my favorite is the poetry I create for Christmas notes, birthdays, or just about any occasion. For example, at one point in my life, a couple of friends decided to give me a microwave. I was touched by their thoughtfulness, and wrote this poem in response:

To my good friends my heartiest thanks
For helping my culinary arts
The microwave oven just fits my needs
No pies or cakes or fancy tarts!

It has just the settings I really like
For popcorn, coffee and pizza too
Help with these tasks is all that I need
The good food here leaves nothing to do.

So once again I thank you a million
You're both as kind as can be
You completed my kitchen
so now I'm settled
Because you both remembered me.

So, if there is a budding writer in you, why not give it a try? When you feel that you have your poem, story or article all ship-shape, don't be shy about submitting it to the local newspaper, a magazine, or even one of several e-zines on the internet who solicit articles, short stories and poetry. Who knows, you just might get your work published!

Even if you are not a computer whiz, old fashioned letter-writing is still a wonderful way to communicate with those we love. I actually greatly prefer receiving a note in my mailbox than an e-mail on my computer. There is just something about handwriting that is becoming a lost art. Phone calls are easier and instantly connect us, but they are over all-too-quickly. In contrast, a handwritten letter can be cherished, saved and reread at any time.

One of the most interesting and worthwhile projects you can invest time in is your family genealogy. With the help of a computer, a printer, and a "big eye" magnifying lens, I spent the better part of eight years putting together a comprehensive history of my family. My grandchildren are surprised and in disbelief when I tell them that as a child the worst thing we could do in school was chew gum! They are always intrigued by the story of our "open" cars complete with transparent eising glass that could be fastened into place by clips in case of rain. It is these precious family stories that should be preserved in a genealogy along with names and dates of birth, marriage and death.

We all probably have more pictures and family memorabilia than we know what to do with. I enlisted the help of one of my daughters in transcribing hundreds of old letters. She thanks me to this day. "I didn't know anything about our ancestors, and I realized that meant there was a lot about me that I did not know," she said. I agree. If we don't know our ancestors' stories, the rich storehouse of resources that they have passed along to us in our genetic coding will probably go unnoticed. All too often we remember only the negatives about some distant relative without looking further to bring the whole picture into focus.

If you've never done a genealogy, look for organizations in your community who will give you some pointers on how to get started. What I found was that once you have gathered all of your pictures, letters, and other documents together, it is best to sort everything you have and put it in some kind of order. Try labeling folders according to decade or year and dropping various bits and pieces of info into the appropriate one. When the material is all sorted, the contents of each folder can then be prepared for permanent preservation. Whenever possible, make notes about events that include the names of any people in photos and an approximate date.

I recently had an idea about an interesting project that might be described as genealogy's "first cousin." I call it a "paper family reunion", because it consists of compiling up-to-date information about every member of a family. The information can be gathered, assembled, and duplicated, and copies sent to everyone participating in the project. Parents can complete the info for children when necessary, and the reunion can include as many people (in-laws, step parents, etc.) as you would like. It's a great project for those of us who have a little extra time on our hands! Questions to be answered could include the usual name, address, date of birth, school or schools attended, major subjects, degree or degrees earned with dates. If a family member is married you could include the date of marriage, a spouse's name and occupation, and the number of children with their names, date of birth, etc. You may even want to ask questions about future plans, hobbies, or other information. It's a great way to get to know your family, even if you cannot meet face-to-face. Moreover, it completely circumvents the issues of travel, time off from work, and finances that so often prevent people from gathering in person.

As you begin to forge out a new routine for yourself, you will quickly discover that the days fly by with increasing speed because you finally have the time to get involved in projects that are fulfilling and exciting. No more "I'll do it another day" excuses allowed!

Chapter 9
It's Never Too Late

The time for action is now.
It's never too late to do something.

Antoine de Saint-Exupery

When I was sixty, I decided that I would enter the work force. Having been at home raising four children for over thirty years, I had participated in lots of PTA meetings and volunteer projects. But I also wanted to see what the business world that consumed so many people's lives was really like.

When our youngest daughter came home from college her freshman year, she found a job working in the office of a temporary employment agency. I asked her if she thought they could find me a job. "Oh, sure, Mom. Just go down and apply," she responded. So I did, and to my surprise, they hired me right away!

I scurried off to my first assignment with excitement but was crushed to find that no one knew quite what to make of me because I was older than the usual "new hire!" But I soon gained acceptance and was cautiously regarded as a "temp."

I went on to quite a few other companies, eventually ending up in the Corporate Trust Department of a large bank. As I started this new assignment, I was a little dismayed with the long computer printouts I was given to analyze. There was a young man working with me who seemed to know all about the job we were supposed to do, so I watched him and pretty soon I caught on to the whole procedure.

One day, the head of the department asked me if I would consider a permanent position with the bank. By now I was pretty interested in all that went on in that department, and the bank was close to my husband's office so we could ride to work together. So, I accepted the job and worked there for almost eight years, eventually becoming an Assistant Vice President until I reached the mandatory retirement age of 70.

I never appreciated the full significance of the old adage "it's never too late to start" more than I did during that period of my life. It continues to be my philosophy to this day, as I am now in my late 80s and still taking on new projects. The truth is, most of us have incredible talents that often for one reason or another we just don't pursue. Isn't the main reason why we don't give things a try because we are afraid of failure? But isn't it worth the risk? What does it mean to "fail" anyway? Doesn't it just mean that we discovered that it wasn't something we really had an interest in anyhow?

I have a grandson who really wants to become an actor. He is bright and funny and talented, but as we all know, the world of acting is highly competitive and somewhat ruthless. One day he asked his mother what he would do if he failed in that profession. Her reply was simple. "I have never known anyone to fail who is as passionate about and committed to doing something as you are to acting."

I think that is the key. Find those things about which you are passionate and pursue them. If you already know what they are, all the better. If you spent much of your life raising kids and putting a roof over your head and food on the table, take advantage of this opportunity to explore.

No matter who you are, what you have done, or what your limitations are, you have a talent. Your challenge is to find exactly what that is, and how to use it. In the process, do your best to meet each day with enthusiasm. That attitude alone will attract others to you and may even open doors you never knew existed. Take pride in who you are, what you have accomplished in your lifetime, and the wisdom you have acquired over the years. You've earned it!

Chapter 10
Slowing Down

The secret of genius is to carry the spirit of the child into old age, which means never losing your enthusiasm.

Aldous Huxley

Eventually, as we grow older we begin to slow down and gradually find it necessary to modify our social activities, exercise routines, and daily chores. We may be a bit more forgetful than in days past, and perhaps have a few more health problems to contend with. We can take comfort in knowing that this is a normal part of the aging process, and it is not necessarily an indication for alarm. By the same token, aging is not a foregone conclusion. Remember that you are as young as you feel!

Someone once described old age as having three stages, young old age, middle old age, and old, old age. I try to stay in the "young old age" category. I just don't feel very old looking out on the world because it looks pretty much the same as always through my eyes!

What the future holds for us will probably depend in part on how physically able we are. Most of us will probably still be fairly active when we move in with our children. So how do we transition to a slower life when our bodies say we must? First, make changes gradually. If your body isn't up for that thirty minute walk, try a fifteen minute one. Eat nutritious foods that sustain your body, especially whole grains, fruits and vegetables. If you have a bad day, don't assume that every day from then on will be that way. Accept what life throws your way one day at a time, and be grateful that you have been blessed with witnessing yet another beautiful sunrise. Above all else, retain your sense of humor, because laughter truly is the best medicine.

From my point of view at that particular time in my life, it was a wonderful feeling to know that all but my personal belongings had been divided up for some time. But there are other important issues to consider as well.

Make sure there are clear records of your finances and investments, and how you want them divided after you leave this world. Do you have a last will and testament? Even if you do, it may need to be updated if you have recently lost your spouse. You may also want to make a Living Will which gives your physician and loved ones permission to disconnect any life-sustaining equipment that may be needed to prolong your life. A copy of your completed Living Will can then be kept with your permanent records and with your medical records in your primary physician's office.

Do your children know where you would like to be buried, and whether or not you prefer cremation? Or would you perhaps like your body donated to science? As difficult a situation as this is to discuss, it is important to do it, and to keep a light-hearted perspective. I remember when my husband and I went to a cemetery to discuss buying a plot, we told the representative (whose name was Mr. Tooms!) that we wanted to be cremated. He laughed and observed, "That's most appropriate for today is Ash Wednesday!"

If you have not discussed each of these points with your children, please do so, especially while you are still feeling hale and hearty. Nothing is more devastating to those left behind than to try to second guess the wishes of a departed loved one who left no clear instructions.

As your routine begins to slow down, if you have been traveling around between children, you will probably want to consider spending time in one household on a more permanent basis, and making less frequent and shorter visits to your other children. Of course the first step would be to see who is willing to consider this arrangement, and whether there is one community where you are more involved than others.

Inevitably, there may come a time when caring for us in their homes is no longer an option for our children. Discuss this honestly and frankly with your children and determine how they feel about it and what your options are. If finances are an issue, determine what resources you can count on from Medicare or Medicaid. It is imperative that you discuss these issues while you are still in good health, so that everyone knows your wishes should a situation arise where you are no longer able to communicate them.

This may be the time when you will need to defer to the advice of your children. You must trust that they are only trying to do what is best for you in the long run, and that you will likely receive better ideas and thoughts with their help than if you had struggled with these issues alone. At that point, you can proudly admire your years of good work as a parent, and happily relinquish that role. I did. And I shall always be thankful for the ten years of wonderful experiences I had with my children and grandchildren who were willing to welcome me into their world and make me feel so at home and a part of their lives. After all, where else could I learn to speak the foreign language of teenagers? To massage my grey matter trying to make sense of a host of newfangled computer games? To span the USA by minivan while running errands with busy daughters? I have learned, and grown, and been nudged to go beyond my farthest boundaries. And thanks to my family, I don't plan to stop now.

Afterword

"Mom, what would happen to you if something happened to me?" my words were direct and somber. "You've got to have a plan-now!" I insisted. We'd been to visit an old friend from Mother's post-college days who made her home in an assisted living apartment in a gorgeous retirement community just a few minutes from my house.

During Mother's lunchtime visit, her friend spoke highly of the amenities available to her—walks in the adjacent woods, wonderful food, a caring staff, and an endless list of activities. I was impressed. After all, there probably would come a time when Mother herself would need some type of assisted living arrangement, even though she steadfastly opposed the idea of a retirement home.

Later that day, I phoned the manager of the property where we had lunch. I wanted to know more about these types of communities, as it was not something I had ever explored in depth. "Oh yes, everyone loves it here," he said. "So much so that we have a five-year waiting list!" I hung up the phone feeling a little bewildered. A waiting list? I'd never even contemplated that.

Over the next few days I discovered that, at least in the communities in my area, there was a long waiting list for entrance. But that wasn't all. It seems that the number of "assisted living" units is considerably smaller than the number of "independent living" apartments and that those assisted living beds are specifically reserved for people who already reside in the independent living community. In other words, if Mom suddenly developed a condition that necessitated the need for assisted living while she was still living with family, she would likely be turned away from one of these communities.

I was concerned. Very concerned. Mom's mind was razor sharp, but her eyesight was continuing to worsen and she had developed a heart condition that caused her to black out on several occasions. It was becoming increasingly clear to all of us that we needed to make some sort of permanent arrangements for her care that went beyond what any of us would be able to provide. Now in her mid-80s, Mother's needs were different than when my father passed away.

For the better part of the ten years Mom lived with her children, she had been in San Antonio, where both my brother and sister reside. During that time, she developed a large group of friends in her church, and had decided early-on that my sister's home would be her permanent address. It was evident that San Antonio would be the best place to begin looking for a suitable retirement community that would be equipped to address the inevitable issues with which we are all faced as our parents age.

I had a growing concern that we were unprepared to handle a sudden decline in Mom's health. In addition to the long retirement home waiting lists that I had learned about, most of the properties in the east, where I now live, carry hefty entrance fees and monthly rates. Without that option, I suddenly had visions of the sort of emergency that would land Mother in some place with the substandard care feared by every older person, not to mention their children. Where would she end up if we were no longer able to provide for her needs?

My oldest sister, Sally, had been considering this issue for quite some time. Shouldering most of the responsibility for Mom's care over the years, she, too, had seen the writing on the wall. But there were also emotional issues on the table, some of which ran very deeply with us kids. Would our mother be happy in the very type of place she had continuously rejected over the years? Would she feel that we had abandoned her? What would our father have thought?

On a hot August day in 2002, Mother fell and fractured her hip while crossing the street. Once again, thankfully, she was spared permanent injuries, but what had been a passing concern for all of us instantly became a constant source of worry. Sensing our unease, Mother herself began to reconsider the idea of some sort of retirement community. In the end, this transition was much smoother than I ever thought possible. Sally located a place only a few minutes from her office that specialized in independent living, with other options available as more care was needed. As luck would have it, one apartment had just become vacant—a lovely, sunny space with a kitchen, living area, bath and good-sized bedroom. The staff was attentive and courteous, and the facility beautifully maintained. I was also relieved to discover that in San Antonio there were no stiff entrance fees and no prohibitively hefty monthly price tag.

Mother seemed more open to the notion than previously, but she still remained skeptical. That is, until she actually visited the property, after which time she enthusiastically embraced the idea.

In what almost seemed like an afterthought, she was moved in and firmly entrenched in classes and projects, meeting people up and down her hall and even welcoming other newcomers. I frequently phoned her only to be told, "I'm sorry, but I've got to go, I'm late for dinner!" The fears I had about her going down hill upon leaving our watch quickly evaporated. In fact, nothing could be further from the truth. I actually think the move took years off her age, and as her children, we are all greatly relieved to know that she is now in the presence of trained professionals should she have any need for assistance.

In retrospect, I look at those years that Mother spent in my home as one of self-discovery, for both of us. She would not have been ready for a retirement home just after my father's death. She needed some time to sort her life out, to ease back into the world without the partner she had lovingly adored for almost fifty years. During that time, we gave her the strength and inspiration to keep going, even if she did not know where or why.

I needed those years as well, not only to learn to relate to Mother as one adult to another, but to be free of the old unfinished bits and pieces that invariably haunt us from our youth, and to see her in a light unobscured by my own emotional baggage.

As happy as she is in her new situation, I know she would never have traded those years with her children, because during that time we all grew in ways otherwise impossible.

On one of her last visits to our family, Mother and I drove to an airport in another city to meet my college-age son and several of his friends. She and I followed their rental car along the interstate as we made our way back home. Ever the comic, my son placed his leg out the window as he drove along. Not one to be outdone, I followed suit. Next, his front-seat passenger joined in. I looked at Mother, she at me, and we knew what had to be done. She rolled down her window, and at age 85, proudly hung her leg out. We both beamed. You see, you never are too old to do anything you want. Thanks, Mom, for teaching me such a valuable life lesson.

Alexandra Rodgers ter Horst
December 2004

About the Author

Margaret Rodgers was born in 1916 in Binghamton, New York. The granddaughter of a Presbyterian minister, her fondest memories are of times spent with family in lively discussions around the dinner table. She graduated with a degree in economics from Elmira College in Elmira, New York, and from there pursued a career that included both the business world and the life of a stay-at-home mom for her four children. She currently resides in San Antonio, Texas.